FROM MOTHER TO DAUGHTER

From _Mother_ to _Daughter_

Thoughts and Advice

on Life, Love, and Marriage

JOAN RIVERS

A BIRCH LANE PRESS BOOK
Published by Carol Publishing Group

Illustrations © 1998 Carol Publishing Group and Zina Saunders
Title page photograph © Ryoichi Utsumi / Photonica
Design by Anne Ricigliano and Lucia Kim
Illustrations by Zina Saunders

A Birch Lane Press Book
Published by Carol Publishing Group
Birch Lane Press is a registered trademark of Carol Communications, Inc.

Editorial, sales and distribution, rights and permissions inquiries should be addressed to Carol Publishing Group, 120 Enterprise Avenue, Secaucus, N.J. 07094

In Canada: Canadian Manda Group, One Atlantic Avenue, Suite 105, Toronto, Ontario M6K 3E7

Carol Publishing books may be purchased in bulk at special discounts for sales promotion, fund-raising, or educational purposes. Special editions can be created to specifications. For details, contact Special Sales Department, 120 Enterprise Avenue, Secaucus, N.J. 07094.

Manufactured in the United States of America

10 9 8 7 6 5 4 3 2 1

Library of Congress Cataloging-in-Publication Data
Rivers, Joan.
    From mother to daughter : thoughts and advice on life, love, and marriage / Joan Rivers.
        p.   cm.
    "A Birch Lane Press book."
    ISBN 1-55972-493-5 (hc)
    1. Marriage.   2. Love.
HQ734.R59   1998
306.81—dc21
                                                        98–42610
                                                        CIP

To my mother,

who I miss more at this moment than ever before.

She knew instinctively what it took me years

of trial and error to learn.

Dearest Darling Melissa,

I am writing this in your old room, propped up on your bed with one of your stuffed animals by my side, and I am crying. I can hear you saying, "Oh, there goes my mother again," but tonight I have a right to even more tears than I shed when you walked down the aisle to get your college diploma just nine months after your father's suicide. Now you are about to walk down another aisle in what will be the happiest moment of your life, and Daddy isn't here to walk beside you, to give you his arm, his love, and his pride when the wedding march is played, and to give you the thoughts a father gives to his daughter at this wondrous time.

And so, with all the love that is in me—an *infinite* amount, my dearest—let me give you some words of my own on the evening before you start your life with your new husband.

As I sit alone in your room, I am looking at the school writing award won by Melissa Rosenberg. I hope I can write as well tonight as that sixth-grader did years ago, for I'm so misty with memories of you, so full of thoughts that I hope will make the years to come glow for you and John. You've already moved out of my house, but vacating my heart is a move you will never make. Yes, here goes your mother waxing mushy again, but, darling, life has never been more bittersweet for me than it is right now. I just wouldn't be human if I didn't feel a little sad. Mostly, of course, I'm so damn *happy* for you as you begin the intoxicating adventure that is married life.

Melissa, the very first gift you ever received came from me, the gift of life; but tonight your birth seems like ancient history, even though you're just twenty-eight. What gift of value can I give you right *now?* Not silver or china or any of the other elegant things that a bride receives from those who love her. No, my first offering to you is intangible, but perhaps the most important thing in anyone's life. It is the gift of *hope.*

As you well know, I'm big on hope, and I am bursting with it on the eve of your wedding, as I sit here writing to that splendid young woman who often knows more than the woman who made the needlepoint pillows that filled our home. Remember all those pillows I stitched while you were growing up? I took my needlepoint work everywhere: to your ballet classes, your school play rehearsals, your swim meets, and all your horse shows. The work kept me busy and happy while I watched you being busy and happy, too.

At first, the pillows were just cute pictures, pillows with clowns and balloons; and then, as you grew older, they began talking about life, with pithy bits of wisdom, like BEFORE YOU MEET YOUR HANDSOME PRINCE, YOU HAVE TO KISS A LOT OF FROGS; YOU CAN NEVER BE TOO RICH OR TOO THIN; the one Bette Davis told me, ALWAYS REMEMBER, BIRDS PECK AT THE BEST FRUIT; and perhaps the most famous one: PLAN AHEAD.

But the pillow that means the most to me followed Daddy's death, the one I made at the end of that awful rift between us. A year after Daddy killed himself, you were graduated from college and I was so deeply proud of you, of the way you had transcended the tragedy to finish school and then had kept going forward to begin a career.

That was when you and I fashioned a precious philosophy together: that passing through life, with its good times and bad, was like acting in an adventure movie with both its highs and lows. You and I, we decided, were the stars of that movie and so we had the power to give it a happy ending. And this is the unforgettable thought that I captured in my final pillow, the one still lighting up my library: WELCOME TO JOAN AND MELISSA'S EXCELLENT ADVENTURE.

That's *exactly* what life is, my darling, and Helen Keller said it so well: "Life is a great adventure or it's nothing." In this exhilarating production, the stars *can* write the script and make much of it play well.

If I had time, I would put other thoughts about your coming marriage on pillows instead of on pages for you, but I don't, so tonight I must needlepoint in print.

The first pillow I would make would say

LOYALTY

Darling, you and your husband John must *always* be
loyal to each other. Through the years, I've admired
your loyalty to your friends, your family, and your
colleagues at work. But the moment that ring encircles
your finger, your primary loyalty must be to only one

Always put the
two of you first.

person. It is the absolute essence of marriage. As the Bible says: "Forsake all others and cleave only unto your husband." John is now the most important person in your life, the one you must care about and defend and help and endlessly love.

You must always *put the two of you first*. Daddy and I used to say that the two of us were a little army, shoulder-to-shoulder against the world, and now the two of you must be your own petite platoon. *Never* talk badly about him to anyone else. Instead, talk to each other about what bothers you and let the world see only a couple happily united.

Pillow two is

COMPROMISE

Of *course* you'll be having disagreements and you've got to air them, but never let yourself become too upset about the little things. When you were small, I used to say, "Missy, save all your tears for when you'll need them. Don't waste them on nonsense." And in life, so *much* is nonsense.

Remember when you, John, and I went to look at silver patterns? Remember the couple who were actually screaming at each other about which patterns they should pick? The essence of nonsense! *Whatever* pattern you pick, whether fleur-de-lis or fig newtons, I guarantee that within six weeks you will hardly notice it again. You know the last time I was aware of the pattern of my dishes? Ronald Reagan was in office!

Never fight over the small stuff—and the small stuff is ninety percent of life. Does it really *matter* whether the den is blue or brown? How about a plaid with both colors in it? You want the bedroom warm, he wants it

Never let yourself
become too upset
about the little things.

cold. Then how about a dual-control electric blanket?
You want to see *Masterpiece Theatre*, he wants a
ballgame. Give him the game. Your marriage is a much
bigger one and you can catch your play on a repeat.
Every marriage has little tensions, and little is what they
have to remain. After the word *love*, the prettiest word
for a couple is *compromise*. You'll lose nothing if you
intermittently let your husband have his way and he lets
you have yours. What gains is your marriage.

It will be only human for you to have bad moods
and even honest arguments with John. But Missy, *never*
misdirect anger at him. Never make him the scapegoat

Never fight over
the small stuff.

for other aggravations. When things are rotten at work or friends let you down or the TV news is a montage of horrors or it's just plain PMS, don't take it out on John. He's the *one* person in the world who will best understand you, the one person who can lovingly nudge your thoughts back into perspective. That's why people get married: to have that beloved other self.

And speaking of the TV news, make *all* your compromises before the news at eleven, for no bulletin will ever be as important as this one: *Never* go to sleep angry. Both of you should say what bothers you and then finish with the happiest non sequitur: "I love you."

Never go to
sleep angry.

Pillow three is

ENJOY THE NOW

Missy, you know I have always believed that if a
person worked hard and behaved well, things would
go right in the end; but the sad truth is that this
isn't always the truth. Though I hate to admit it,
God's divine plan for mankind includes a dismay-
ing amount of incomprehensible randomness.

You probably know that melancholy saying: Man plans, God laughs.

I don't have to tell someone as intelligent as you that terrible things happen in every life—and they happen to *everyone*: no one's life is without its times of darkness. Last week when we were in the beauty salon, we saw women with perfect hair and clothes who looked as though they hadn't a care in the world. But if I had asked each of them, "Has there ever been a time in your life when you said, 'I just can't get through this. You've got to help me, God'?" I am telling you right now that each one would have said yes.

And so, darling, *because* people go through truly bad times, *enjoy* the happy ones and never let them be spoiled by petty foolishness—or major foolishness either. Young married people may fight over the colors of their carpets or the makes of their cars or whether they should vacation in Aruba or Asbury Park, but such matters fade to nothingness when a real crisis comes up.

I know a husband and wife who fought fiercely over whether the new house they were building should be split-level or colonial. And then the wife developed breast cancer. Suddenly where they would be living didn't seem to matter, for they weren't sure if she would *be* living at all. What a heartbreaking lesson in perspective!

Bad times pass, but the good times do, too, so savor the good ones as deeply as you can. I hope you and John will always enjoy the now, will always be aware of all the good things that both of you are blessed with: youth and health and friends and energy and hope. Try to remember that little poem I've always loved:

> *Yesterday is history;*
> *Tomorrow is a mystery.*
> *Today is God's gift;*
> *That's why it's called the Present.*

Be aware of all the
good things that both of
you are blessed with.

It's such a simple sentiment, but so true. Delight in the present, darling. Savor all the moments of happiness that the two of you have *as they happen*—like sunshine pouring through the windows of your home the first time you sit together in your breakfast nook. The first night in your new bed. Your first dinner party. Be aware that these are the good times that create your treasured memories. The bad times never pass unnoticed, so for God's sake, make *sure* you give your happy ones equal attention!

Every night in my diary, I write three good things that happened to me that day, a literary exercise I

Savor all the moments
of happiness . . .
as they happen.

strongly recommend to you. There are so many small blessings we so often take for granted—like the first snowfall of winter, when the city is freshly white and people suddenly seem more friendly. Or bumping into an old friend you're delighted to see. Or being able to afford a new book you want to read instead of waiting for it at the library. Or the sweet tranquillity of dawn, when a new day with all its promise lies before you. It's all in your attitude, darling, so make it one of perspective, appreciation, and delight, and never, never postpone your joy. Be aware as it happens. Know when you are living the good times.

Pillow four is

BE THE WISE BAMBOO

There are so many clichés about marriage: how it is
endless compromising, how you have to keep learning
to give and take, how you must not expect to always
have your own way. Well, they are clichés *because* they
are true.

Of *course* you won't always get your way with John, but so what? Marriage isn't a contest to see who is most often right. Marriage requires your being what the Japanese call "the wise bamboo," which means you bend so that you don't break. Treat your husband not only with love but with flexibility and the respect you would give to a top client. Think how businesspeople treat their clients: They smile, they're polite, and they listen to ideas, seeking a common ground in order to move forward. Never forget that John is your most important client.

Treat your in-laws with that same respect, too, for they can become lovely friends, or they can be difficult for you. Your husband's parents love him as much as I love you and probably think no one is good enough for him, just as I think no one is good enough for you. Remember that they were the stars of his life long before you took it over, and it does hurt to be dropped to second place. Be as gracious with them as I expect John to be with me, for I've also dropped to second spot.

However, don't let your in-laws walk all over you. How you run your house and cook and decorate, *how you raise your children,* are the business of only you and your husband! Your life is a play that *nobody* is allowed to review. In this play, continue to be your own person

and don't let *anyone*—John's mother or father or me—
tell you how to live, because the only authorities on that
subject are the two of you, period. It is *your* life, so live
it with *your* decisions.

Pillow five is

OPTIMISM

And now a huge cheer for optimism, not always hip but such a good way to look at life. Damn those people who, upon hearing of a wedding, say, "Well, let's hope it works." Yes, America's divorce rate is fifty percent, but that means fifty percent of all marriages *succeed*.

Look at it *that* way rather than starting out mentally dividing your property. If you both really *want* this marriage to succeed, if you work at it and play by the rules, then in a union as strong as yours and John's, happiness can be a self-fulfilling wish. So buy that sofa you'll have to share throughout life rather than a sectional that can easily go two separate ways.

Of *course* your relationship will have lows, but you don't have to be Plato to know that you can't fully appreciate the highs without the lows. People on the equator, where it is always summer, never know the beauty of spring and fall, And so, as the seasons of your marriage change, savor them—and hope for no hurricanes.

Pillow six is

SEX

Now see me change from mother to girlfriend. I'm not sure that a mother talks to a daughter this way, but this is how I would talk if one of my best friends was getting married—and my best friend *is*.

In a good solid marriage sex counts.

Procreation is our basic mission on earth (once we are finished shopping), so always keep yourself attractive for your husband if you can. Remember how you looked when you were courting? All those cute little outfits, with your hair just right and your makeup perfect? Remember all those pretty panties and bras? Well, don't put them in storage just because you're married. Don't slip too deeply into old T-shirts and torn jeans.

Physical attraction is what brought you together originally. We are part of the animal kingdom and one of our basic instincts is responding to that magnetic appeal.

Birds have their mating calls. You have Victoria's Secret.

A male friend recently said to me, "Tell Melissa to forget about buying furniture. Tell her to go shopping for sexy underwear." Darling, John may now be your husband, but keep him your lover, too.

Never forget the erotic part of the fall that your husband took when he fell in love with you. Your body is your temple, Melissa. Keep it that way so that he'll always want to worship there. Never take this lover for granted. Always try to remain the alluring girl he was so attracted to. I know that days will get hectic and time for leisure will be hard to find, but my mother taught

He may now be
your husband,
but keep him
your lover, too.

me this, and I pass it on to you: If there is a choice between looking good and doing the laundry, look good. No man ever made love to a woman because the sheets were pressed!

Of *course* you love each other for your minds and hearts, but *both* men *and* women are constantly driven by lower zones—and that's great: hooray for sex! *Enjoy* it. Relax, be adventurous, and try everything. The term *consenting adults* means just that. Let yourselves qualify for that *new* expression: *Been there, done that.* Make sex a happy, exciting, intimate game played by the two of you.

And when the children arrive, you and your husband

must try to keep taking a day or a night just for your-selves. Go to a hotel if you have to and lose yourself in romance, in sensuality. There's a song that asks, *How do you keep the music playing?* It is up to you both: you two are the whole band.

The next pillow says

HUMOR

Knowing how you and I have lived our lives, I don't know if this pillow is even needed, but it's message can never be stressed enough.

Laughter is very special. God gave it *only* to mankind. Think about it. We are the only species that is able to laugh.

And so, use this gift often and laugh whenever you can, because laughter will be almost as important as love is in pulling you through. You have always been able to laugh during life's darkest moments. Remember your first prom? You were looking so lovely in your strapless dress and your date arrived wearing white cotton gloves. You rushed up to your room in tears and I went up and convinced you that white gloves were perfectly proper— for a dance at Tara. You laughed and came downstairs and told him the same joke. *He* laughed and took off the gloves, and away you went, you in bare shoulders and he in bare hands.

Remember our dinner in that restaurant a couple of weeks after Daddy's death? It was our first time together in public after his funeral and you were so lost and so broken that I couldn't even recognize your sweet face across the table. Then I looked at the menu with those stratospheric prices and said, "Missy, if Daddy saw us paying these prices, he'd kill himself all over again." You laughed, and for a moment I saw a heart-lifting return of the face I cherished, brought back by humor.

Most healing processes begin with laughter. Laughter kept your father and me going for twenty unforgettable years—until, tragically, he stopped laughing. And now I hope that laughter does the same thing for you and John for fifty years at least.

Major pillow time: one that simply says

GOD

As you well know, Daddy and I were raised in the Jewish tradition and that's how we raised you. But now you're about to marry an Episcopalian. Everyone keeps telling me, "Times have changed. The world is smaller now and all traditions are blending into each other and that's fine."

But *is* it? I don't know. What I *do* know is that as long as both of you believe in a Supreme Being who wants all of us to love each other, protect each other, and be compassionate with each other, maybe it doesn't matter how you connect with Him or in what building you make the connection.

My only melancholy thought about this Judeo-Christian wedding is that some wonderful customs may end. Will you celebrate Passover and Chanukah? Will you observe Yom Kippur? Will John continue to celebrate Christmas and Easter? I hope that *all* the holidays will come into your home and that the two of

A belief in God and
a feeling for religious
rituals will help bond
your marriage.

you will forge a strong religious chain for your children and theirs, one that says: God is great and we reach Him joyfully in many equally valid ways. A belief in God and a feeling for religious rituals will help bond your marriage. I pray that you and John will always have this celestial glue.

Pillows are meant to support us and to keep our heads comfortable. And I think that, for you and me, mine have done just that. The next pillow, however, is the one uncomfortable one:

DEATH

Although this letter is intended to celebrate the wonders and joys of your new life, I must remind you that, just as the moon has a dark side, so does life, and it is called death.

It still breaks my heart whenever I think how young you were when you were forced to learn how the death of a loved one changes everything forever. However, whether such tragic loss enters a life sooner or later, it *will* happen, so try to be prepared to accept it, grieve, and then *move forward.*

I truly hope you will have no more brushes with death until my own. When that time comes, you must remember that this will be in the right order, in nature's wise plan as it is memorably spelled out in Ecclesiastes: *One generation passeth away and another cometh.* Yes, this is the proper pattern of life, the plan for the evolution of the species. And yet, no matter how right it is, when you lose someone close, the way you lost Daddy, the pain is almost beyond bearing.

My own mother and I were as close as you and I have been. In fact, I never called her Mother, I called her Bea because subconsciously I guess I thought of her as my closest girlfriend. When she died, even though I had a devoted husband and a wonderful daughter named Melissa, I truly thought my life was over.

My mother had great taste, and there were things of hers I had loved and wanted to have all my life. But as her possessions began to come into my home, I realized that I didn't want her things, I wanted her. All those tables and dishes and linens no longer represented beauty and taste. They represented loss and pain. I couldn't bear to look at them, and so I packed them away for many years.

As time passed and I got some perspective about my loss, I realized that these objects collected with such love by my mother were not to be shunned but to be used with delight. They represented a continuation of her. My enjoying them was a loving memory, a direct connection to her; my pleasure in them continued the bond between us.

Some day, Melissa, the things I've loved will be loved by you and John and then by your children. And these things will contain the message that those who have died continue to live as long as their things are remembered, used, and loved by their descendants.

Many people feel that death makes a mockery of life, makes it pointless and absurd. I feel just the opposite: The existence of death actually *heightens* life and makes it something to be savored every minute. Birth and death are the natural progress of the world, the endless renewal of the planet, and both of them must be appreciated as part of the wondrous cycle that the Bible speaks of so poetically.

The existence of death
actually heightens life
and makes it something
to be savored every minute.

Whenever the latter part of this cycle takes a loved one from you and John, my darling, always remember that the human heart is our strongest organ, for it is indomitable. The musicians are right: *The beat goes on.* There *is* life after pain, after loss, after death. And no matter how dark things become, sunny days and laughter always, always return. God will help us to turn the page to begin the new chapter.

And now for the pillow less grim than Death and less
happy than Humor, but just as meaningful as both: the
pillow that says

MONEY

What financial advice do I have for you and John? First,
don't listen to the people who say money doesn't matter.
It does. As you surely remember, I've been rich and
I've been poor—in fact, two or three times for each—

and my only lesson comes not from Alan Greenspan but from another noted economist, Mae West, who said, "I've been rich and I've been poor, and rich is better."

In the bad old days, the man worked and the woman stayed home. Today, you and John are equal as wage earners and the wages you make will be important. Don't let people tell you that money means nothing. If they feel that way, tell them to give you theirs. Money can't buy happiness, but it does bring comfort to you and those you love. It *is* a handy way to buy food and fix a child's teeth and send your son to Yale—or your daughter to Barnard.

Your money is for you and your family first. However, anyone lucky enough to have money should find a way to share some of it with those in need. I cannot stress this too strongly, darling: *Every one of us has to give something back.* If a person is lucky enough to do well, then she *must* lend a hand to those who need a lift. I think that's why God gave us money in the first place.

Never forget, my darling, that no matter how happy you are, no matter how good life is to the two of you, always stop to understand your finances. Don't make the

Lend a hand to those
who need a lift.

mistake *I* did. I was so naive about finances that after Daddy died, it took me a while to figure things out, to understand what we had, where it went, and most important of all, how to conserve it.

Please, please, please do not get complacent, do not get lazy. Always remain open to opportunities to make more money. Things happen, Missy. The only predictable thing in life's fortunes is unpredictability. Husbands fall ill; businesses change; stock markets tumble. And so, keep yourself abreast and ready to move on to new avenues. Self-sufficiency is freedom. There is nothing more satisfying than to be able to pay your own bills.

The joy of being
self-sufficient is one
of life's sweetest candies.

The joy of being self-sufficient is one of life's sweetest candies. And never, never feel that any work you do to keep you and your family alive is beneath you. Which brings us to . . .

The next pillow,

PRIDE

This is the only pillow that should have a footnote embroidered on both sides, saying SEE OTHER SIDE, because there are *two* sides to pride.

Side One: We all have been taught that pride is important—pride in our achievements, our appearance, our children—and this pride is the good pride.

PRIDE*

*see
other
side

However, turn the pillow over and see the other kind of pride, the kind of pride that is self-defeating. If you have professional or financial reverses, never be afraid to take *any* job that comes along. There is honor in all work. God has given us arms, legs, and strength; use them. *No* honest work is beneath you.

After winning a Tony Award, the great Judy Holliday was asked by a producer to audition for a new show.

"Judy, *you* don't audition," said her agent.

"Why not?" she replied. "It's only humiliation."

Judy was right, but she just said it wrong. What she

There is honor
in all work.

meant was: there is no humiliation in doing something to achieve an honorable end. And if you live by this code, then *that* is something to be proud of.

Melissa, I just realized that unpredictability isn't life's only constant theme: There *is* one other: change. And so, it is fitting that the last pillow should read

CHANGE TOGETHER

The message of this pillow may be a bit disturbing, darling, because you feel that you and John are perfect right now—and you *are*.

However, even in the glow of the lovely rapport that the two of you have, you must remember, in a tiny corner of your mind, that people change and so do relationships. And yes, that means they can get even *better,* but only if you both learn to appreciate the newness that will keep coming from each of you.

Marriage is—I hate the word—*work.* Of *course* it's a joy and a comfort and a haven for you both outside your careers. But you also must work to keep up with the new interests that each of you will be developing through the years. As you did when you first met, try to develop interest in things that interest him. Make an effort to stay tuned to his life. You may not love basketball, but he'll be delighted if you know what a "backdoor play" is. You never want your husband leaving *your* door—front or back—to find people more on his wavelength than you.

And once you are married, remember the little things that actually make up the heart of life: What he likes to eat. What music he likes to play. What trips he likes to take. Keep being considerate of each other, for each of you must always remain the most treasured guest in the house of the other. The happiest sentence spoken each day should be "I'm going home now."

The happiest sentence
spoken each day should
be "I'm going home now."

I just realized that I don't need the lamp anymore to see what I'm writing. It is now almost dawn. My God, Melissa, it's your wedding day! In just a few more hours, the hairdresser and makeup lady will arrive and the bridesmaids will be calling and there will be hysteria because the shoes haven't come or the limo is late or we'll discover we are two waiters short. There will be last-minute instructions and adjustments. And then, suddenly, before we're really ready, one of your old college friends will offer me his arm, take me to my seat, and the wedding that you and I agonized over and planned so many times for so many months will begin. John and his best man will step out from the side of the altar, and your dearest friends, in the dresses that we hope will make them all look beautiful, will come down the aisle past me two by two.

And then the music will stop, there will be a pause, a hush, and next the strains of the wedding march will stirringly sound and all the other guests and I will stand and turn, and you, Melissa, will appear in the doorway. And yes, I'll start to cry because you look so young and radiant and vulnerable, cry because this is the end of our long chapter together, cry because you will be coming down the aisle on the arm of your godfather instead of the arm of Daddy. My tears will flow freely because, on this day of days, when the rabbi asks, "Who gives this woman away?" it will not be Daddy's voice sounding out a loud, clear "I do."

But remember that the glowing bride coming down that aisle, Melissa, isn't just *my* daughter moving toward the altar but your father's daughter, too. Behind you are his parents and my parents and their parents and their parents' parents, on into infinity—couples that came together on days just as glorious as this one, days as filled with hope for their futures as today is filled with hope for yours. All their love and good wishes are wrapped tenderly about you because, in the flow of time, they *are* you. And so, as you go forth, you are representing all of us.

Oh, my darling, there is still so much to say from my strange new position outside your life. I'm so happy to see where you're going with John, but it is hard for me to accept my smaller role. For the last ten years, Missy, you and I have been such a lovely team: alone together, as the song says. It has been just the two of us: not merely mother and daughter but devoted friends and confidantes. We are two people who have flown around the world just to be together for holidays. But now your flight's destination must always be John.

Darling, I love you beyond words and I want your whole life to be as beautiful as it will be in this one shining ceremony. How fervently I wish that I could spare you any pain forever—but of course I can't. All I can do is give you these thoughts and hope that long after I'm gone, you will still remember a few of them and they will help you as if I'd been there to lovingly say them to you.

And so, I'm releasing you, my darling, not that you knew I even had to. I'm releasing you to replace me now as the most important person in your life. Your husband is now the center of your universe, just as you must be the center of his. You are the sun in your new world with him, just as he is the sun for you. Don't ask me how there can be two suns. Every marriage has a certain wondrous mystery, a private splendor that forever remains inscrutable.

Every marriage has a
certain wondrous mystery,
a private splendor that
forever remains inscrutable.

And now, I send you my blessings, darling, at the start of Melissa and John's excellent adventure.

I love you with all my heart.

You are my heart.

Mommy

ABOUT THE AUTHOR

Joan Rivers is one of the hardest-working women in show business—comedienne, playwright, screenwriter, motion picture director, nightclub headliner, Emmy Award–winning television talk-show hostess, and, most important, a mother. She is the author of *Bouncing Back* and six other books, including a number of bestsellers. She lives in New York.